Flightless Bird

Rosemarie Corlett

Flightless Bird

Shearsman Books

First published in the United Kingdom in 2022 by
Shearsman Books Ltd
PO Box 4239
Swindon
SN3 9FN

Shearsman Books Ltd Registered Office
30–31 St. James Place, Mangotsfield, Bristol BS16 9JB
(this address not for correspondence)

www.shearsman.com

ISBN 978-1-84861-830-5

Contents

For Ella

ACKNOWLEDGEMENTS

Thank you so much to Miriam Darlington, Min Wild and Angela Smith for your support, love and care in making this poetry collection a reality.

Some of the poems in this volume have previously appeared elsewhere. My thanks to the editors.

'I'll Invent and Emu', in 'Flightless Birds in Contemporary Poetry'. *Responding to Creative Writing.* Harper, G (Ed) (Cambridge Scholars Press, 2020)

'Ladies Kindly Remove Your Hats', in 'Flightless Birds in Contemporary Poetry'. *Responding to Creative Writing.* Harper, G (Ed) (Cambridge Scholars Press, 2020)

'Margot Don't Travel'. *Finished Creatures* (Corrupted Poetry, 2020)

'God is an Ostrich'. *Lighthouse Journal* (Gatehouse Press, 2019)

'Snowy Owl', in *Owl Sense.* Darlington, M. (Guardian Faber, 2019)

'The Glimpse'. *Poetry Wales*

'Paper Bird'. *Poetry Wales*

'Karen Carpenter on Drums in the Azaleas'. *IOTA – The Outsider* (Templar Press, 2018)

'Preparing Game Bird – Notes to Self'. *Thief* (Tribe Media, 2016)

Preparing Game Bird – Notes to Self

mix sugar, syrup and bicarb in a deep saucepan

while she bubbles, shrink a good tree (if you don't have a whole tree,
      the bonsai's fine)
cover the shrunken tree with slabs of the hot toffee mixture

                                      {as though making
leave to cool   Papier-mâché
carefully remove the branches from inside the cinder toffee casing

when the honeycomb frame feels weightless in your palm, you know
      you have the skeleton *

for the feathers:

julienne a bridal veil then iron out the splay with starch
break off a high heel for the centre spine of each plume
have a friend play a continuous tremolo on the violin to get everyone
      in the mood for flight
if you run out of wedding train, flatten a pompon and comb out its
      threads
hook the barbs with corset eyelets to resist the wind- <u>ruffle</u>

next, assemble:

— any pocket you ever kept conkers in   4 CHAMBERS

— a burnt out lightbulb   OF

— the envelope from a letter you still keep
            in its envelope   THE HEART

— a heart shaped balloon

cover your hands in bitter, dark marmalade

wind up angel hair pasta like a ball of yarn to make the brain

place it against the keyhole on a windy day so she starts to get a taste
            for breeze

make the legs
lock the legs
(so that it doesn't fall off a branch when sleeping)

get up early, go outside and hold her
good
make it last before it goes
then hold her up into the half light

* if it's still any heavier than a box of matches, fill it with sound
absorbed by books until it begins to coast a little on your skin

Karen Carpenter on Drums in the Azaleas

Your body is the half-second before thunder
                    when air is cleaned.

Without its breath-cushion
the outside world is binned electrics and unpredictable lasers
                              planted in the ground
                                        over time.

                                        It's itchy

and unsustainable

but you weave the sediment poles
and master your sticks
like a slalom skier.
And you can get to the core of the earth

even in a small garden.

                    When you get to the very centre
(which can be anywhere)
you surprise a wild animal there –
                    it's rude and brief and for me it's a bird but it's only
the wildness that's important.

A circus poet once told me that the thing she loves most about
birds is that they're constantly in their essence. So listen,

I want you to know,
you hit that for me.

And I know it's real

because your drums spread through the garden like blood moves
through snow.

The beats got right in
the interstices of the crazy paving,

                               seeped into the wood of the bench,
                    filled the garden gnome's eyes,
                         coloured the contents of the water butt
                               so rain came out pink.

                It felt like a bouncy castle inflating around me,

and the moon,
breathless,
blew it up
through a telescopic straw – an unseen aliveness –
    like when roses relax overnight.

Paper Bird

There is a moment
in the folds
when the paper torso resembles a cut diamond,
        or a gutted pig.

From here I bend the sides
like breaking buffalo wings
and cave in the neck with my thumb
to make a reverse
face.
Once assembled, the body
is a live riddle. I hope

        that someone robs a bank
     in the time it takes to make this bird.

Time speeds up
when you build a flightless afternoon. My thief
sweats –
     the soft hair on the skin of his heart.
Closing his hand
around hunks of soft banknotes cut
like hair –
     from the safe to the bag to the car.

Don't move,
he says. Hard to say why it's delicious
except to mention that my friend Emma
touched down on the same mood once:

> *Flew to Vietnam to have sex in a parked car*
> *with a man I met online,*

the postcard read. She met him there
in that place where *don't move* means *move,*

a little.

Crime

is a paper bird.

I hang it with cotton string and watch it slowly spin. I'm reminded
of a story
where children thought a rabbit
they dug up was alive
because it moved around in water. Their teacher
placed a stick in the stream to teach them something.

Margot Don't Travel

The hanging cage by the tumble dryer
is pregnant with a bird.

She grows inside it like a foetus
or a finished book being annotated.

She lives in a red brick house
that is pregnant
with a floral room
and the damp room is pregnant
with a birdcage
and the antique cage is pregnant
with a caged bird.

And inside the yellow bird
is a beating heart
and the heart is like the bird
because it can move but cannot travel.
      Margot Fonteyn is dancing
inside the old TV set –
the bird-heart ballerina
whose pirouettes go nowhere.
The growing bird learns one word:

Margot. She calls it like *Mother*
over and over, making a different cage

with words. She says it
inside a hundred layers of skin.

God is an Ostrich

No one strapped the feathers to her back, careful
to glue the plumes in even numbers
either side, so she might sit true and weighted
and understand the nature of justice. No,

she rose under my heart the Ostrich-god –
a kinky book under a mattress, the loaded daydreaming figure
glimpsed between two prison bars –
all the interstitial stuff, mixed up and left

to rise a soulful voice that does all the spaces
between the notes. Her mute body-song left a moon-clock
under the stairs. We'd sit there and uplight
our faces with a torch, the little door left

oblique and ajar (ostrich tells time by casting a shadow
over one of an infinite number of torch-lit eyelashes).
She was sultry, even then – the liminal space between two types of
          weather,
when the elements go backstage and get creaturely – ostrich

only comes in an electric space of absence. I want to press a word
into being the way she traces divinity for fun in the sand.
With her formidable weapon-legs – robotic tree trunks

writing cursive stream-code all over the earth,
like a sea tractor might write the word *crazy*
in joined up writing on the beach. Her waxy eye, big as an orange

or a second trimester foetus – how must the landscape
look to her as she charges through the physical world, sparking
fountains and negative lightning with her beaming, flightless charge?

Ladies Kindly Remove Your Hats

Don't put me on a pedestal
because I will let you

down. I wear a plumed hat
to a silent film – the violence

of a feather draws close
to my body. Dense and bound,

amphitheatred with oranges,
the headdress blocks

the movie screen –
balanced erect with imitation

deadness; I'm no use
                    to fauxweathers.

    It's probably that I'm trying

to provoke a murder. *My* murder
flicks across soft millinery, bang
against the auditorium. Bedeck me

good in meteor crêpe –
she bought it to be looked at –

my bad
    heart, yes

arranges like a story. Or bordering collected
stories, asleep on each other's shoulders:
one a waxed clementine,

next the lacquered feather of a flightless bird.
I'll have it all at once
and one at a time. And the insides.

Not the Sort of Thing One Gives a Name

The sublime figure
    of a jumbo jet: at once fat

and incomprehensibly athletic.
    Too big for a child

to look at really.
    I tense my eyes into slits

as we step inside the plane.
    Sat down breathing

baked-bean-air, I drift
    and decide that there are words

inside words
    (like love is inside the word clover) –

they're stuck but they flutter,
    like moths in jars. And they crawl around the in-flight magazine –

soft bodied fireflies
    with glow-in-the-dark organs: one flash

a broken Christmas light,
    the next a compressed musical. Because

I won't see our garden again: so big
    it stretched past snack time. All the way down

to an empty
    sunken pool, lounging

in mustard leaves. Three metal steps down
    to no water. My sister

and I, bare
    skin on the concrete, so young

our feet are still opening out
    in little blooming fists:

twenty curly toes being flattened and educated
    in the ways of being flat. I left

my fingerless gloves
    to the mustard tree, because

I was rushing
    and I hadn't given them names yet.

Flightless Bird

you take me to that place you like where paintings are prenatal and
développés of colour and oil extend up the chairs and flick up the
door and the vulnerability all over your kiss gives off its own imaginary
nationality silenced through language with a rich and muted culture
your lips wear like an emblem when you order coffee beyond you there's
a flightless bird lingering in one of the canvas' abstractions mincing in
and out of sight like a cat she reveals to us with her silenced wings and
magnificent body that useless and fully realised are the same thing I
came across when I found a hair inside my ex-husband's Bukowski book
from when I wore it long and curly when I'd mastered the colour codes
on baby food and knew all the buttons on the pram I closed the book
with shameful care and nestled it between two hardbacks knowing my
old hair inside my ex-husband's book of poems is a maquette for an
unrealisable project and the unbearable quantity of shatterable models
bleeds off on me like the cabin pressure of your lips' biography and the
broken bird all sex before it's converted into this hyper present rings
with both hands ecstatic flash at the frontier between the imaginary and
your physical touch me in the doorway of a black box installation

Funk Island

The light is reliably strange here,
hand-held at the brink of evening

civil twilight. We crack
through leaves for days to find it,

feeling out Funk Island:
faithless enough to hold volumes

of bird fables. To the forest that's juiciest
underfoot, to catch the glossy
instructions in the dirt:

    How to Take Off

a pamphlet tucked inside a Snickers wrapper,
or curled around a string of pearls. The pages full

of tightly wound words like *costive, splint* or *gravadlax.*
Words that sit on the tongue like tablets, and begin

to feel tantalisingly unruined.
We pour hot water over all the ink,

cross out the rest, then spread the gaps
with sprawling, aerated words,
like *spurned* or *treacherous* or *holocaust*.

The Menagerie

A flotilla of Great Auks
embarks off the skerry;
birds plucked for feathers and boiled
for oil. We build
two canoes the shape of
two crescent moons, fill them with rocks
to keep them upright, and cross the sea up and down
the rookery, until it's too dark to see.
For the journeys back, the rocks are replaced
with the same weight in shoulder to shoulder
dead birds. It's cramped when we inflate
the Great Auks' windpipes, attach them
to bladder darts, and make harpoons, to kill more, perhaps.

It's because it's the year of the animal.
Like the royal menagerie's
black-crowned heron,
its boney stork and sexless flamingos,
these sickle shaped cages full of flightless birds find
weary elevation in pictures and pendants. Oeuvres
brightly ringed
by concertina wire and you can smell it – the warehoused
seeking asylum – sketched, spun,
sculpted, debated – this sudden presence
of a collection
of recorded animals – one of their bodies, clothed only

in dark pants and socks, was left on a breezeway
        for two hours. Wrapped in baggy lemon skin,
            the bodies laid down.
                Eyes up or aslant – no more glare-blind
                    than water, each slips
                        back and forth between the islets.

We Killed Two Flightless Birds

I understood later
that the birds matched a pair of coal eyes
I had pressed into a snowman in my family home.

You take one real thing out of the world
but you don't know which imagined thing shares its coordinates.

And when we clubbed

the birds for real in the world, two floating black eyes
were scooped from a soft white drawing.
I awake

from a nap where snowman faces make no sense
and go outside to check the cemetery is still the same.
Relaxing my eyes

over the rows of grave crosses,
it's like the swathe of bumblebees that emerges
when you adjust your focus on lavender flowers.

And this levelled field of wooden crosses
becomes a field of scarecrows, stripped and arranged open armed in
the sun.

The hot force
reserved for hammering guitar chords
graduated to something more sibilant that morning.
They were so tame

when we killed them; it felt like undressing a scarecrow.

Prophet-like that Lone One Stood

A section of low cliffs
    sunk in
by caves and natural arches.
      Papa Westray –
          where bird feathers
      fill pillows.
    The sac of stone painted pink
could be mistaken
      for a bouquet of thrift in the sea-haar.
But it's the Great Auk.
      It stands on the cliffs of Fowl Craig,
gentle cairn, made by children
  in the shape of a bird.
Beaks strewn
      over maritime archaic coast;
this auk is made of rose stone – all wrong,
        a concrete mute
    and yet still
    a tremendous effort of exactness
pushes forward
    like sex:
      the desire to resurrect,
      energised by anxiety.

You weigh the same
      as a 6-month-old and you will not withstand
any psychic slackness.
              And you embody
     a wholly private language –
        like meeting a baby,
      seeing you is an act
       of seeing
and of being exposed
      at the same time. This daft scrum of pink
painted sea stones –
            anarchic even at its most canonised;
your small body will bear
      terrible inspection. And your nutcracker beak
        will be with the unheard.
In summer, your plumage shows
a white patch on each eye: two eggs. Twins.
              Exotic
    animal capital. In winter you lose the patches,
instead developing a white band
        stretching between the eyes.
   A charismatic icon of extinction,
        with unseen stealth.
Your body will only ever be known
        by water.

Leda and the Ostrich

When you rub your neck,
                    sneeze,
          or drink coffee,

some banality
          beacons my body
into a temporary moon – furious
          and far-reaching
as the bat-signal.

It happens
when I write your name

in condensation.
          The beam is strong enough to change
a painting in a gallery,
          a Type A oeuvre like Leda and the Swan,

     into something breathtakingly bastard: half-blood
          gorgeous, treacherous lovely mongrel
sexy fresco and oils where plaster

forms a physical bond
          with paint. And the painted swan

becomes an ostrich. And all

      the gallery birds go monster – a camel-sparrow neck

snakes around Leda where a swan once stood:

this is the pull of your honeytrap mouth on the lip of a cup.
I search my body until I know it's illegal

and Leda skirts a bird-beast in a painting in a gallery.

Immediacy

I liked it when you said the word *immediacy*
because the clock

and me listening and your knuckles near my legs
all met the word and held it locked. I don't know

to what extent these moments of fluke exactness
occur. If they're rare, I'll save them

for you.
I find you exciting burning up my letters –

it was a similar day I must have swallowed words'
hold: that push and juice and gesture. I know

because I was sitting on my hands
to stop shaking. Later

I'll hear the shard of a song
through the closing door of a commercial kitchen:
the backs of your fingers along the soft side
of my arm. Bad heart
speculation yields so fast –
your mouth was a wave leaning back into its momentum.

It's when you're radiant this way with different paint
on your callus fingers that things

       section off. Like all the sprawling
absent nights I've watched people have sex
    with me were scrupulously ordained
        to appear
in stunning contrast with you pulling my hair.

Fabric

The urge to rip the bedroom air in half is met with a vision.
          Spreading all the clothes apart inside the wardrobe,
I think of nothing
but fabric – the hangers' concertina racket
   as I push inside the clothes,
the draft's easy exhale through linen shirts.
          Fake fur unbreathes,
itchy and electric and there's
                    discontinued
fragrance stuck in the fibres.
The hanging outfits look like a queue of cartoon characters.
                         In the way cartoon characters'
               paunchy arms
and clashing clothes
          merit no
          particular notice.
It's as though their fluorescence and blindness to physical pain
are the manifestation of an internal might – the same
                              deep declaration
                         that beams inside
                              blues singing –
the steel anvil
     inside the ostrich's throat.

                    The duck down inside
a hanging quilted jacket handles like a stress ball,

and I knead the breast feathers
tucked within the nylon pockets. And I think
        of Donald and Daffy Duck playing that Hungarian Rhapsody,
their duelling pianos rasping like two knackered lungs,
                    smashing out some blessedness
with their arms and legs and beaks,
                and it feels
                like a frenzied and vital
opposition to all the years I went home,
                and drank coffee standing up,
and did the dishes before turning on the radio,
                and rejected my husband's advances
        as if all pleasure must be paid for.
I'd like all this stuff to fall on me

    from a great height – hot pink taffeta
on giant leather and sheepskin bent off
                the copper wire hanger. That this wardrobe might function
as the opposite of a portal: a place to be smothered
in pantomime clothes,
                    the sneezing thump as they come down together,
            the slipping sound of one arm off a hanger,
then later the other – and the wardrobe floor would relent,
and receive
        its troupe of collapsing ghosts.

Go as Slow as You Can
and Do Everything You Want

the disco lights
make palm trees look like fireworks
   staring into the eye   of the tree's boom
is like moving
through two parallel fields   on the top deck of a bus,
(where backwards
    and forwards
are the same)
       or being born

you could feed acres of soil
   then fire a gun   with the volley
of unmet desire in the world   wasted
    eroticism into a curtain
of fire and longing
will now appear backwards
historically   like time before the birth
of Christ   a countdown rewinds

I'll Invent an Emu

I'll spread out an ostrich, then shrink its frame.
Until it's tall as a man, comely as a girl,
and beefy as an emperor penguin.
I'll humiliate its bones then dress its feet

with bustard or burnt quail slippers.
I'll tend to a cassowary's triptych claws,
and slip the bird four working bellies.
I'll call its song a straight blues drumbeat,

un-render bush medicine and the oil from lamps,
cut open soft capsules to set its cushy fat in motion,
uncurl a ball of string to substitute its tendons.
The steak knives will assemble into the shape of its skeleton,

while its meat slowly grows the same ph. value as beef.
The blue moon will come. All the way down to earth
without rolling or adjusting or getting any bigger.
And an egg will land as softly as a cat

inside my emu's nest. I'll tuck in my arms and claim
I was the first to be flightless, then steep a 747
in imbricate petals. I'll roll a beluga in soot and scales.

I'll ask that we look up to the dark cloud lanes
when the Milky Way is clear and dying, and I'll demand
we see an emu reaching out for itself in a trail of running dust.

St Kilda

1.

I only see her picture, but it feels like looking at a photo
of myself as a child – her carriage so much more sober
than the other extinct birds.

Where the red rail arches its talons, and the little bittern
pouts its chest, the Great Auk holds no internalised mood.
No anchor to herself. It's like she's waiting

to ask permission. She is black on one side
and white on the other, like a sea stack at sunrise.
I love her dark hair against the white dress.

She models herself: a sexual bride with instant history,
a moving story, if stories become moving
the moment their contents are released.

Extinction – the hand that just now held a gold coin,
opens up and vanishes.

2.

I love to imagine the family prayers
spoken softly for the last time –
the delicious black image
of a bible left open in each house.

We boarded a steamer for the archipelago
of St Kilda, to obtain a postmark
before the island was evacuated.
Later that year, its inhabitants

were gathered and removed.
It's a scene that begs

the same terrific yearning
for a storm so severe
it leaves you deaf for a week.
For the island bay's conflicting winds
to see a dozen sheep blown over

a cliff. For the timbre
of the seabirds' screamings –
the one remaining unmuted frequency,
to unlock the weather and foreshadow
its decisiveness. To be free
yet to freely espouse

an island fit for prison,
fit for good impartial justice – the factor
dressed in a long tweed trench-coat
beside the heap of harvested gannets.

3.

Before humans vanished from St Kilda,
there was a golden hour
in which their paucity was rehearsed,
with seabirds enacting the dry run
of what it means to be flatteringly scarce.

Each year, the Great Auk
slipped ashore to lay one egg
on bare rock. And as the value
of her diminishing body increased,

her single egg came to function
like a postmark: a collector's record
timestamped in the dark – inkless,
mineral and freeform.

It wasn't difficult for the three islanders
who found her asleep.
These were the same alpine cragsmen
who hammered bolts,
fastened ropes around their chests,
scaled barefoot to better grip the familiar,
soaking descents. The same men
who years later would pay in felt and oil
for their own evacuation.

4.

They caught her asleep and for three days
the Great Auk hovered, like witchcraft –
pre-liminal and blaringly realised
with her legs tied together.

As a storm reached its bleakest
they beat her for an hour. Broke her
short sleeves with two large stones,
then placed her behind the bothy –
each shaking with the extraordinary heat
of touching a family member
as she goes. Later, dead gannets

were slipped through the gaps in their belts,
and their bodies snowed occasional feathers
on their way back up the rock face.
By evening, they had cleared a fulmar roost
so dense it blanched the rocks,
gently dismantling
the seabirds' concrete poem
to open up a path along the ledge.

Flight

It was an accident.
A twinjet
and a duo of giant birds,
ingested,
one down each engine.
    First, bang into the blade root,
second across the nose cone.
And the plane slips

and falls
into a stately home.
Always the most unruined thing,
trashed.
And so
a mansion with a jet though its middle,
and all the branded napkins
up in a flurry,
the seats' under-foam all showing,
a big house full of seat belts
    and relatives.

ONLY GARDEN BIRDS AND THE FAMILY BUDGIE SURVIVE

Underneath the papers, there is a brochure on the doormat.
It reads:

6 hours 55 minutes to Europe.
You sense the difference
when you step aboard a bird.

On the phone table
just inside
is a bone china bowl of sweets,
  wrapped
    one at a time.
They would have smelled
and tasted
that peculiar floral sweetness,
like violets.

Out the stain glass, the nanny's ghost
pops out
in the topiary patterns,
        billowing out
picnic table linen
and the house sparrow's breasts
      inflate
and give off talc.
      Look up! she gestures
A tin goose is skywriting.

It's incredible, joined up in smoke:
      there's no message
an advert or a proposal perhaps.

The Glimpse

Then you'll pass an archway
that looks through to the parking lot,
and a ghost will slip through.
Something about the heat

or arrangement of the cars –
it whispers to another
unnoteable instance
where objects were mapped like this.

The cars are plotted as far and deep
as dinner plates one summer.
Two hanging baskets: a hologram
of your parents on the balcony.

The depth of cloud
against a slanted clay roof
and the rhyming of streetlights
send a flash of childhood holiday,

followed by an unnameable sadness.
And you sleep all afternoon
to downgrade the longing.
And you panic when a leaflet

falls out the newspaper later,
aware that going a day
without encountering childhood,

is like trying to spend a day
without seeing

or hearing
a bird.

Snowy Owl

A crystal note alighting
on the Cornish tundra,
you bring news
of the next glacial blowing.
Coded in your feathers,
an address
with no letters and no numbers.
Moon fatale.
You spread your wings
so there's no shade
between your feathers.
I press my cheek against the edges
of your flight feathers
and feel like my heart's breaking.

The Word Kiss

You look so good stood up.
    To lie you down
would be
to fell a tree, your face
encrusted with your eyes. I kiss
the word *kiss*
in a book to calm down. You place

a conch shell to my ear –
    Sounds like the dark
driving through rumour
in the realest pretend things.
Some knowingness, yes,
the grey breath in the shell
is the edge of sleep. The torture

of being a personality –
    you upturn an answer,
an aperture in the hell of it.
And when that happens
it is immediate love. My ears

exhale; you read aloud.
    And somewhere else,
marching songs

relent to the floor,
and use their feet like hands.

Dodo

My skull rests
in the oldest zoo
in Copenhagen.

Believers lick their lips
behind the glass
at my brain's cradle,

and chew over who
could have arranged me
this way –

dysfunctional.
The ungodliness
of a flightless bird,

they prattle.
She has
no working wings.

Just three or four
black feathers
branded nastily

either side,
to mark
where wings aren't,

and to imply
that she broke a promise.
Wet descriptions

can be found of her
in wrecked ships' journals.
Each log

reads a little different,
but they always end
the same –

    Note:
The longer I am cooked,
the less tender I become.

I want
  to know my tail plumes
may
smell of ash.

I may be
      um
sexually dimorphic,

and my biology
may mis-sell
levitation like a joke,

but my design is full.
As natural and legitimate
as a free bird.

There are seventeen of us left.
Dozing in a swamp
covered with hard core.

A flight
of grounded beauties
holidayed

under concrete,
sat tight for years.
We love to imagine

white bones enmeshed
in the trees and palms
along the bay

where explorers have died
and disintegrated
trying to reach us

for a kiss.
I keep a handkerchief
from one of the ships

with the words

                Hurry Slowly My Love

sewn into the cotton.

To be one of your things

There's a plane
        draped over the beach.
Wings out, on its front – a toddler napping,
                three windows missing.
And the very tip of its nose
might be gone.
It's no beast

in silence like this;
the sun
draws dark circles
under two white wings – a miscarriage.
I don't wish

to do anything again.
        Especially help.
        I realise now
with brut salience
        that I was never, ever born
to be useful.

Spit

The stream at your sides
slips away
in one soft, disappearing arrow,

as though your chest were sharp glass
parting liquid glass. As long

as you're alive,
there is a closed door

that holds a roomful of water.
I'm sorry the scars

on your face
come up like snowflakes –
like the pattern of a ballet corps

seen from up in the gods.
Without wanting, your whiteness
shunts my ponytail,

and spit-shines my eyeballs.
And it's all I can do
not to watch you all afternoon,

going, going
with your athlete's curves
and your glaring sad function.

Emus in Winter

Your bodies encourage the mountain range to climb
and gather snow. A balsam fir tail, dense with brown needles,
curves and assures the deep valley of your neck.

It is as though each small part of your body
signals something larger. A single blade of grass
hangs from one of your beaks.

The Collector's Egg

Its shell is smothered in calligraphy.
Like the writing inside the curly paper
that holds up cocktail umbrellas,

or a cave turned inside out
with all its crevices un-indented.
Morse code's uprightness melted down –
riddled with pores so a chick could breathe
two hundred years ago.

It engenders the same feeling of flatness
as when you open a drawer of butterflies –
        the anti-climax,
even if they're abundant
and teemed and the colours are good.

Barely an egg, it rolls about in the seat
of an unusual generosity –
        a strange largesse
to gesture to your own obsolescence.
Too assured to be historical,
it holds a yellow eye,
holds nothing,
holds the absence.

Tracks

In real life, the male emu squats on his eggs.
But somewhere else, a new man moves thickly
from out of a tall impersonation –
              the waves wring out his ankles.

He makes the coastline and the inland desert.
Digs with a conch shell to reach water, leaving impressions
of his body and his efforts on the earth. Cupped leaves,

set like offering hands, simper down
and alight inside his footprints –
           many cradles within a larger cradle.
He leaves
behind the grooved impressions of his tail feathers,
like the markings of a pheasant who has been walking through snow.

Perhaps he is half-emu, half-God,
but this separation
        is as illusory
as the gated-ness of the real emu's incubation. The whole

story gives way to a further offing to admire
and take fresh solace in –
             all the footprints
continually weaving
illegible confessions extending, extending

along the coastline. Then installed in one of the earth's depressions,
a new chick, cream with brown stripes,
hatches from a dark green egg. The Indian Ocean
creeps up the full moon, sky-clear season staircase

of satellite wrinkles up, up across the ocean.
An emu. Within
        its new nomadic family, following floods to feed.

Perhaps she is being mindful,

resting her eyes, transforming her life.
It is an oblique loneliness to watch someone this way.
Inside the lining of this loneliness is a picture of myself on a train.
I once sat next to a woman on a train
who was old with a young face, like a model from the sixties –
wholesome as eggs. And you could imagine her frying eggs,
in her eyeliner and the orange tint photos had back then.
And the feeling of this train's drive in my body
is muscular and deft and ungainly and very good
in the way heavy birds are often very good runners.
In the way strange looking animals are occasionally protected
in a symbolic way – roughly lauded for their unusual bodies,
appearing on postage stamps and such, a vague emblem of resilience.
On the train I am free in this way – a still shot of potential movement.
What a person might look like just before something changes.

The Crying Room

There is a small room in this church
called the crying room.
A place to take howling children
who disturb the Sunday service.

A small flock of rooks
flew over the room this evening.
Their flight sounded like a waterfall,
audible through the unlatched window.
Water rushing down
through anchored rocks
like still air gushing through birds –
as if the world had turned on its side
and a breeze had been
poured through their wings.

I know what it is to lie
because you have never been believed.
How there is an oblique
and panicked integrity
to even the lowest of deceits.

This room can hold the tension.

A slow, deep place
for the rooks to beat their wings

slowly and deeply.
A different kind of flight
thrashes under the breastbone –
urgent, serious applause
trapped inside a handkerchief.

I walk home and run a bath.
And when the taps are full and going,
I put my head completely under;
I can hear the crying rooks.

CPSIA information can be obtained
at www.ICGtesting.com
Printed in the USA
BVHW081427300922
648391BV00008B/1565